Text Styles

Text Styles

Consistent Work Flow from Word Processor to Page Layout

Henrietta Flores

DAGMAR MIURA

LOS ANGELES

Published by Dagmar Miura
Los Angeles
www.dagmarmiura.com

Text Styles: Consistent Work Flow from Word Processor to Page Layout

First published 2022

ISBN: 978-1-956744-73-6

Contents

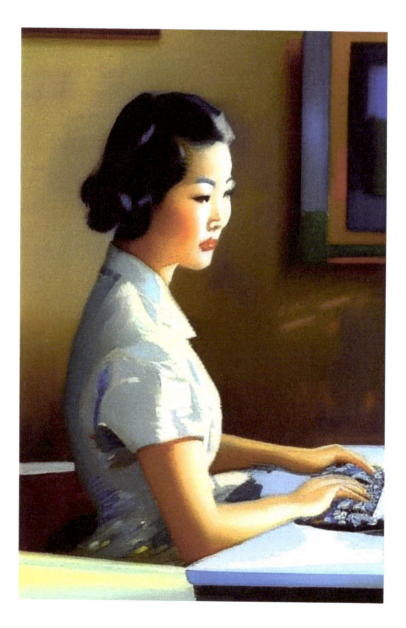

Introduction

Books and text-heavy documents typically start with a writer using a word processor and end up with a designer who does layout using a design program. How do we maintain a consistent work flow from the typing-it stage to the final design? Major publishing houses and the media arms of big companies have invested in all-in-one systems, start-to-end packages that streamline the production process and get everyone on board using the same standards.

Corporate outfits with resources on that scale don't need my help—**this guide is for smaller entities like freelancers or individual publishers who want to get projects organized and keep things clear.** If you're a designer who works with a variety of editors or writers to create print or digital documents, this guide is for you. If you're a writer or an editor who wants to produce the tightest manuscript possible with a minimum of back-and-forth ambiguity with your designer, this guide is for you.

All the information contained herein could be gleaned from the documentation that exists for word processing software, layout software, and text style systems. You could also watch the many instructional videos that are sure to exist online. This guide is aimed at written-word people—those of us who prefer to learn by reading rather than watching videos. My aim with this guide is to set out the process of using text styles from word processing to page layout, transcending the specific software ecosystems.

One caveat about the contents of this guide: most of the software discussed herein uses the subscription model, which means the programs are continually updated for stability, with new features, and to work with revised operating systems. It's likely that over time, some of the procedures and features I've described will work slightly differently, and revisions to the programs might obviate some of the steps. Even though the details will inevitably change, the big-picture understanding of text styles that I've laid out should be valid for quite some time.

The Issue

When creating a book or a text-heavy document, how do we maintain the creator's intentions for the various parts of the text as the project moves from the writer's work through the designer's?

- For **writers,** how do we clearly lay out our intentions for the various text elements before we hand over the manuscript to an editor or designer?
- For **editors,** how do we sharpen the writer's intentions to make them clear for the designer?
- For **designers** doing the layout, how do we understand the text elements of the project without resorting to guesswork?

The answer is **text styles.** A text style is a named collection of formatting attributes that are applied to whole paragraphs and to individual words and characters. The handy thing about text styles is that they are built into most of the software we already use in publishing—you don't have to buy anything or pay additional subscription fees to make use of them. Even better, there are libraries of text styles you can access for free that are comprehensive and cover any conceivable text formatting need.

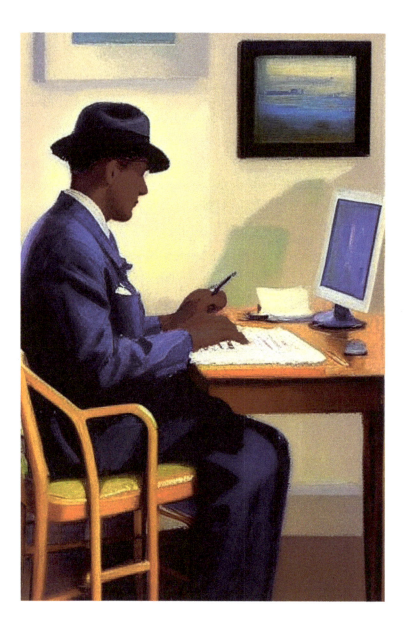

Why Text Styles

Who is this guide for?

- **writers,** who can assign text styles when creating manuscripts
- **editors,** who can assign or revise text styles when editing manuscripts
- **designers,** who work with text styles to streamline design and layout

If you're creating or editing a manuscript for an established publisher or a client with a lot of experience, they may tell you what system of text styles to use, even providing a template that contains them. If you're working with a freelance designer, they may have text styles preferences; don't hesitate to ask. If you're a designer who gets a text document formatted with text styles, making full use of them will save you hours of guesswork and text tweaking. Read on for guidance in these situations.

Why do we use styles?

Casual users of word processing programs usually just employ **direct formatting.** They format paragraphs and words manually to apply attributes like the font family, font size, boldface, and italics. In a layout program, designers who haven't learned to use styles might go through a document and format each paragraph individually. Using text styles instead means we shift our thinking from *what the text looks like* to *what the text is.* Applying text styles empowers creators to clearly show what each part of the text is intended to be, and allows designers to understand these intentions.

Direct formatting

Most people who write using word processors don't bother with styles. Word provides other ways to get the text to look the way a writer wants it to look. Writers can easily change the font and the size of the text, and they can click on Word's B and I buttons to make the text look bold or italicized. But all this formatting is only an overlay—it doesn't apply a character style or a paragraph style.

In the same way, typing five or six spaces at the start of a paragraph doesn't impose an "indented paragraph" text style, and typing a long series of carriage returns doesn't create a "chapter title" text style, even though editors and designers might be able to deduce that those are the writer's intentions. Styles have to be added independently of the word processor's direct formatting.

Intent, not design

In the design stage, the document designer will determine what fonts to use, what point size the text will be, and what the headings and sidebars will look like. For writers and editors, what matters is the intent of each part of the manuscript. The details of the actual formatting don't matter in the early stages of creating a manuscript, but the intent always matters. Using text styles allows us to mark each part of the text to be what it's intended to be so that there's no ambiguity later.

Writers don't usually work with styles. Editors and designers often receive manuscripts where every line bears the "Normal" text style, and thus the intent is vague. A writer might format the chapter titles by centering them, and an editor or designer might understand the intention. But are the first-level subheadings the ones the writer put in boldface, or the ones in 18-point type, or the ones in italics? Does three carriage returns mean that's the end of the chapter, or was the writer just trying to get to a new page?

If we use text styles, the point size and font and spacing don't matter because chapter titles, for example, will bear a text style that means "this is a chapter title." In different systems this text style is called **Chapter_Title** or **Chapter-Head** or **ct**. The word processor might show this text style as boldface or not, in green or in black, in 14-point type or 20-point type. What they look like doesn't matter, as long as the intention is clear—meaning that they are marked with the chapter-title text style.

Likewise, regardless of how they appear on the screen, the top-level subheadings will be obvious when they are styled with a text style that means "first-level subheading," with a name like **H1** or **A-head** or **ah**. Everyone down the line who looks at the manuscript, in a word processor or in a design program, can see the text style names, and there is no ambiguity about what each paragraph is supposed to be.

In the layout program, the designer can then easily tweak the attributes of the text style itself, changing the font and size and spacing. Rather than revising each individual chapter title, adjusting the text style in a layout program like InDesign applies the change to all the text marked as chapter titles at once.

What are text styles?

To reiterate, a **text style** is a named collection of formatting attributes that are applied to whole paragraphs and to individual words and characters.

Two kinds of styles

A **paragraph style** is applied to a whole paragraph. A **character style** is applied to individual characters, words, or phrases. Paragraph styles indicate things like "This is a chapter title" or "This is the first paragraph after a heading" or "This is a regular indented paragraph." Character styles indicate things like "These words are italicized" or "This word is boldface" or "These characters are an internet link."

In Microsoft Word and other word processors, the **Styles pane** shows the text styles contained in the document. Paragraph styles and character styles are listed together, differentiated by a symbol to the right of the style name. In this example of the Styles pane, Normal is a paragraph style, marked by the pilcrow, ¶. Bold and i are character styles, marked by **a** . image and outline are combined paragraph and character styles, marked by the pilcrow and "a" together: ¶a. More

about the use of combined styles appears below in "Working with combined styles," page 35.

In the layout program InDesign, character styles and paragraph styles are shown in separate panels. The **Paragraph Styles panel** at right contains the styles imported from the Word document in the example above. The paragraph styles that were imported are image, Normal, and outline. The symbol to the right of the style Normal, ⤓, means the style was imported along with the text but hasn't yet been adjusted in InDesign.

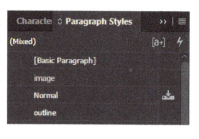

InDesign's **Character Styles panel** shows the character styles imported from the Word document. Bold, i, and url were in the Word document, but notice that two other character styles have been generated from the combined styles, in Word marked as ¶a. image Char

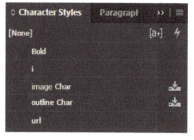

contains the character formatting of the image style, and outline Char contains the character formatting of outline. Both image and outline also appear in the Paragraph Styles panel. Word displays the styles as combined, and InDesign has split them into separate paragraph and character styles.

In both word processors and design software, the styles panels are ground zero for text styles: you can see what text styles are already in the document, and you can quickly apply a style—just select the text in the manuscript, then click on the name of the text style to apply it.

Text style collections

Microsoft Word and other word processors have extensive built-in text styles, but they aren't specifically calibrated for publishing. Word has text styles like Emphasis and Salutation and Signature, which might be handy tools for civilians writing term papers and interoffice memos. In publishing we need a different set of text styles—for a paragraph that includes a drop cap at the beginning of a book chapter, for example, or text styles for photo credits and image captions, or text styles for different lines of poetry.

InDesign doesn't have built-in text styles, but you can easily create new text styles. It makes sense that there aren't any predefined text styles in the layout program: those should come with the text when it's imported into the document.

It's possible to use a word processor's built-in text styles to format a manuscript for publishing. It's also possible to uncork a wine bottle with a screwdriver, but why would you do that when there are more precise tools at hand? Text style collections specifically designed for publishing have already been created. They aren't necessarily free to use or readily accessible, and most collections fall under somebody's copyright. It's also possible to create your own set of text styles, but why reinvent the wheel? There are robust systems available that you can use without a subscription or a license.

You might find your client is already dialed in to one of these existing systems. Publishing houses often have their own text style collections set up for specific purposes, like publications that have an idiosyncratic look: a collection of text styles for cookbooks, for example, or a collection for travel guides. Two widely used collections that transcend individual companies and projects are **Happenstance** and **Scribe**.

If someone in your work flow is attached to a specific system, ask them for a template that contains the styles and for documentation about the collection. If you're working with a publishing business that has an established set of text styles, they will have templates and documentation to hand to you.

Scribe's ScML

Scribe sells a beginning-to-end publishing system called Well-Formed Document Workflow that covers every step and every possibility in document publishing. If you work for someone who has access to that, dive into it—you won't need this guide. Part of Scribe's system is a collection of text styles called ScML, the Scribe Markup Language. Scribe has created extensive documentation for these text styles as well as Word templates that contain all of the ScML text styles, freely available online.

Scribe's intent in making ScML freely available, rather than protecting it behind a paywall or a subscription, is likely that they want to make the system more ubiquitous in the publishing world. If freelancers and small entities like us are able to use it freely, that will build on Scribe's visibility and market share.

My job isn't to interpret or defend someone else's copyrights, but common sense implies that if a tool is freely available from the creator on the open internet, they want you to use it. ScML is a well-rounded and well-conceived tool, with over eight hundred individual text styles. If you're not already using a specific collection of text styles, snag ScML and make full use of it. Your warm feeling of goodwill toward its creators will surely help grow their business in the future.

ScML template: A page with templates that contain the ScML text styles: https://scribenet.com/wfdw/resources

Click on "Word Template" to download a zipped file. Don't open the template, a document named scr-word-template.dot. Just pull it out of the zipped file. We'll make use of it later without actually opening it.

ScML documentation: A web page that concisely states what each ScML text style is used for: https://scribenet .com/wfdw/docs/scml.html

What software are we talking about?

A variety of publishing software and support software have text styles built in, or have support for text styles built in. This guide deals mostly with two eight-hundred-pound gorillas in this field: Microsoft Word and Adobe InDesign. A rundown of some of the software used in the publishing work flow:

✓ **Microsoft Word:** Even though most writers don't even notice, Microsoft Word has robust built-in support for styles. Microsoft wants Word to be a universal tool, so it provides the easy-to-use direct formatting for casual users who just need the printout to look right, and also supports a more technical system of text styles for professionals like us. Word has been developed over many decades, so it has evolved to work quite smoothly in the publishing work flow.

✗ **Google Docs:** Docs is a nifty free tool, but it doesn't support text styles. In fact, I would label Google Docs as publishing kryptonite: If you use Google Docs to edit a Word document that has been formatted with text styles, Google Docs will actually strip out all the text styles and replace them with direct formatting, then save it as the same Word document. When you look at the document in Word again, or when the next person in the publishing process looks at it, every paragraph will bear the text style "Normal." This is a work-flow disaster—the writer or editor would have to go through the manuscript and reapply all the text styles, or the person doing layout would have to guess about what the text is intended to be.

✓ **LibreOffice Writer:** Writer supports text styles, and applying them is similar to Word, with a Styles deck that resembles Word's Styles pane.

✓ **OpenOffice Writer:** Writer supports text styles, with a Styles pane, and has a lengthy list of built-in text styles.

✓ **Scrivener:** supports text styles, with a pull-down menu and a Styles panel to manage them.

✓ **Apple Pages:** supports text styles, with a pull-down menu and a Styles panel.

✓ **Adobe InDesign:** Text styles are fully integrated.

✗ **Quark XPress:** Quark XPress was at its zenith in the 1990s, and the last time I saw it in use would have been around 2005. But corporations are slow to evolve when it comes to software that works well enough. Even though it's theoretically possible to import a Word document or a rich-text document with the text styles intact, my reading implies that it's a difficult process, as the program prefers an older system where individual text elements are tagged with text codes. Making text styles work with Quark XPress is beyond the scope of this guide.

✗ **Scribus:** The program can import paragraph styles but not character styles (the difference is explained above in "Two kinds of styles," page 7).

✗ **plain-text editors:** Programs like **Notepad++**, **BBEdit**, and **TextPad** are designed to edit plain text, not for word processing, and they don't support text styles. These programs are incredibly useful for coding—they can render the commands in programming languages and languages like HTML and CSS in different colors, and can clearly organize the structure and layers of code. But they're not useful in writing or editing a manuscript.

Using Text Styles in Word or Another Word Processor

If the manuscript you're writing or editing doesn't already have a set of publishing text styles included, you can copy a set of text styles into the document. The process is explained in detail below, but to summarize:

1. Import the set of text styles into the manuscript you're working on.
2. Configure the word processor so that you can easily see the text styles and work with them.
3. If necessary, tweak the text styles to make them more writing- or editing-friendly.

If your client or designer has a specific set of text styles they want you to use, ask for a template that contains them. Any Word document (.docx) or Word template (.dotx or .dotm) can contain any number of text styles, as can documents in generic rich-text format (.rtf).

From this point forward, I have to focus specifically on Microsoft Word. Other word processors like OpenOffice Writer, LibreOffice Writer, and Apple Pages should be able to handle text styles in a similar way, but to get into granular detail, I will describe how things work in Word.

The look and feel of subscription-based Word 365 seems to change slightly on a regular basis, but the fundamentals of working with text styles won't change. The same results are possible at least as far back as Word 2010, even though the steps to get to the same goal might be a little different. In each case I'll explain the goal, so that you can figure it out in your version of Word, when I outline the precise steps to take for Word 365.

Also, the keyboard shortcuts I describe should work the same on a Mac as on Windows, if you replace the CTRL key with the COMMAND (⌘) key and the ALT key with Mac's OPTION key.

Templates with macros

Your client might send you a Word template loaded with all the system's text styles, but it might also be loaded with macros that format text for you. Scribe and Happenstance, for example, have both created text style templates for Word. For both systems, I've heard writers and editors complain that these templates and the process of learning the macros are cumbersome and counterintuitive. Personally, I'm leery of anything like this that requires me to install software and learn a new microsystem. If you're comfortable installing the template and learning the macros, go for it! If you're not up for doing that, **you don't have to use the macros.**

Using text styles without the macros

All you really need to create a perfectly styled manuscript is the text styles themselves, not the template and the macros that impose them. A simpler way to work with text styles in a manuscript is to use only Word's built-in capabilities to manage text styles. One big advantage to using Word's system is that in future, if a publisher or a client asks you to work with a different set of styles, you'll already know how to do it— only the style names will be different, and you won't have to learn a new set of macros.

1. Import the text styles into the manuscript

You'll need to have the Word document or template that contains the set of text styles available on your computer. You can tell the difference between an ordinary Word document and a Word template by the file extension: .doc or .docx are for regular documents, .dot or .dotx are for templates, and .docm or .dotm files are loaded with macros. If you've downloaded the ScML text styles, as described above in "Scribe's ScML" (page 10), it's a file named scr-word-template.dot. In the Happenstance system, the template is named something like HappenstanceSD.dotm. Don't open the file; just be aware of where to find it.

1. First, open the manuscript you're working on.

2. Open the Styles pane. Word has several windows or panels where you can view and interact with text styles, in Word called "Styles." The most prominent, called the Style Gallery, shows up as a ribbon under the Home tab, but it's not very useful. The one we need is called the Styles pane. Open the Styles pane by clicking on the ⬍ button at the lower right of the Style Gallery ribbon, or open it with a keyboard shortcut: CTRL+ALT+SHIFT+S (hold down the CTRL, ALT, and SHIFT keys at the same time, and type s). The Styles pane usually pops up to the right side of the main window. You can anchor it on that side by dragging it to the right, and then adjust its width if necessary.

3. Import the text styles. The Styles pane shows text styles in list format. It might show you all the styles in the document, or all the styles the writer or most recent contributor has used, or maybe all the styles in the known universe plus all the direct-formatting overlays, depending on how your copy of Word has been tweaked and what any other writer or editor has done with the file. Often it's a big mess. We'll tidy it up later, but first, let's import the text styles:

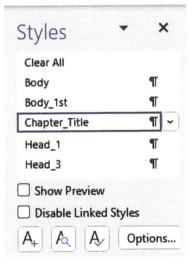

- At the bottom of the Styles pane, click on "Manage Styles": the button is a capital A with a green checkmark on it, $A_✓$.
- The Manage Styles window will pop up. At the bottom left of this window, click on "Import/Export." A window called "Organizer" will pop up.

In the Organizer window, the pane at left shows all the styles in the manuscript you're working on. The pane at right shows all the styles in an external document, probably Word's built-in global template, called "Normal.dotm."

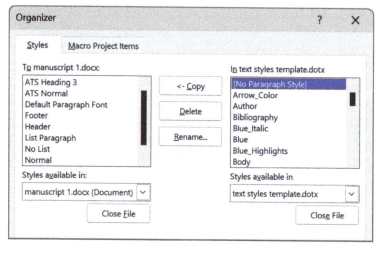

- On the Organizer's right pane, click on "Close File." The right-side list will disappear and the button will then change to "Open File."
- Click on "Open File." An Open window will pop up.
- At the bottom right of this Open window, click on the box that says "All Word templates." This will bring up a list of file types.
- Choose the "All Files" option, the first in the list.
- This Open window shows your local files. Locate the document or template that contains the text styles you want. If you downloaded the ScML template, it's a file named scr-word-template.dot.
- Select the file and click "Open."

The right pane in the Organizer will now show all the text styles that are contained in the template. They are listed alphabetically. In the ScML system, the first few will have names like "ah" "au" "b" and "bh." In the Happenstance system, the list starts with something like "BackMatterAbout-TheAuthor" and "BackMatterTitle." This list is the text styles you want to import into the manuscript you're working on.

A template should have only the intended set of styles in it, but other types of documents might have more. Depending on how the file has been used before, there might be some unneeded leftover text styles in the list. I see a style named "apple-converted-space" appear often, for example. The list also might contain some or all of Word's built-in default text styles. None of these extra styles will have any impact on the overall use of text styles, so you can import them along with the rest and just ignore them later.

- In the right pane, select the first style in the list by clicking on it; it will now be highlighted.
- Scroll to the bottom of the list of styles, then hold the SHIFT key, and click on the last style. The entire list will now be selected and highlighted.
- Between the two panes, click on the button labeled "< - Copy." This will copy all the text styles from the template into the document on the left side—the manuscript you're working on.
- If a question box pops up to ask "Do you wish to overwrite existing style entries?" Just click "Yes." The result might be that the appearance of some of the text in the manuscript will change. For example, Word's "Normal" text style uses the font Calibri in some versions of Word and Times New Roman in other versions. This sudden change in appearance can be alarming, but it doesn't change the content of the manuscript. Remember that the way the text looks doesn't really matter—you're going to be changing the appearance anyway when you apply the new text styles.
- Close the Organizer window.

This process allows you to copy all the text styles from

any Word document or template without actually opening it or installing the macros that the template contains. From now on, you can work with the text styles using only Word's own capabilities.

2. Configure Word so that you can easily see the styles and work with them

To work with text styles, first open the Styles pane, as explained above at "2. Open the Styles pane" (page 15).

Next, you can get Word to display the paragraph styles for each paragraph in a column alongside the manuscript. This is called the **Style area pane,** and it is positioned to the left of the document's text. Using this pane speeds up working with text styles a lot, but it only works in Draft view.

1. Change the view to Draft. Usually Word displays documents in Print Layout mode, emulating on your screen what a paper printout would look like. Draft view lets us see things differently.

- Click on the "View" tab at the top of Word's main window. At the left side of the ribbon are the "Views" options.
- Click on "Draft."

As a side note, if you don't already use Draft view, it's also useful for editors reviewing changes to a manuscript done with Track Changes turned on. Print Layout view usually displays text deletions off to the side, where it's not easy to visualize them, but Draft view shows all the text changes more clearly, right in the text. The trade-off is that it's harder to see Comments in Draft view.

2. Turn off Draft fonts. In Draft view, your version of Word may suddenly display everything in a typewriter-style font. The document's formatting hasn't been lost, but we have to tell Word to show the formatting the same way it looked in the Print Layout:

- Click on the "File" tab at the top of Word's main window.
- Near the bottom left, click on "Options." The "Word

Options" window will pop up.
- In the list on the left side, click on "Advanced," then scroll down to the section titled "Show document content."
- One of the options is "Use draft font in Draft and Outline views." Uncheck this box.

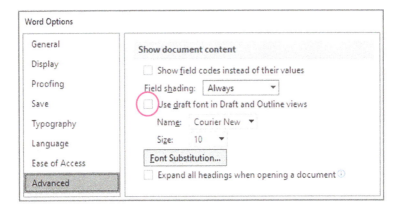

3. Open the Style area pane. This is also achieved in the Word Options window.

- Click on the "File" tab at the top of Word's main window.
- Near the bottom left, click on "Options." The "Word Options" window will pop up.

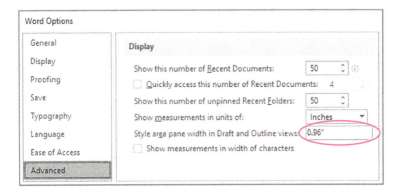

- In the list on the left side, click on "Advanced," then scroll down to the section titled "Display."
- One of the options is "Style area pane width in Draft and

Outline views." Type in a number greater than zero. This number is the width the pane will be. One inch (type 1″) works well to start.

- Click "OK" at the bottom of the Word Options window.

The manuscript should now display the Style area pane, a column at the left side of the text that lists the paragraph style for each of the document's paragraphs. You can adjust the width of this column by grabbing and dragging the line that separates it from the text.

Each time you open the manuscript, Word defaults to Print Layout view, so you will have to manually switch to Draft view again. But once you are in Draft view, the Style area pane should still be visible.

4. Adjust the Styles pane to display the list of text styles clearly. Back in the Styles pane, most likely positioned on the right side of the main Word window, the list of text styles might be very simple or might be a lengthy jumbled mess, depending on what other contributors have done with the manuscript and with the template you imported the text styles from. You can change the way this list is displayed to make it easier to work with.

- At the bottom of the Styles pane, click on the button labeled "Options." The Style Pane Options window pops up, shown in the image below.
- In the list of options for "Select styles to show," the two useful choices are "In use" and "In current document." When you're starting work on a manuscript, choose "In

current document." This will show a list of all of the text styles that you imported, plus whatever was in the manuscript previously.

Later on, once you've started to apply the text styles, you can change this setting to "In use" to shorten the list and show only the styles you've already applied, instead of showing every available style.

- In the list of options for "Select how list is sorted," choose "Alphabetical."

The next part of the Style Pane Options window shows three checkboxes under "Select formatting to show as styles." When these boxes are checked, the list includes all the direct formatting or overlays. For example, if the writer wanted to mark a paragraph as a block quote, they might have used direct formatting to increase the point size and then to add boldface. In the list of styles in the Styles pane, this might appear as "Normal + 14 pt + Bold." "Normal" is Word's default paragraph style, and the "14 pt" and "Bold" are not styles but rather direct-formatting overlays.

- When you're starting work on an existing unformatted manuscript, uncheck all three of the "Select formatting to show" boxes. This will shorten the list by hiding all the direct-formatting overlays, so that the list displays only the base style names.

3. Tweak the text styles to make them more editing-friendly

One of the useful aspects of text styles is that it doesn't matter what the exact formatting looks like. As long as the text is labeled with text styles, everyone who looks at it after you can see what the chapter titles are, styled with **ct** or **Chapter_ Title**, and which paragraphs are a numbered list (**nl** or **List-Numbered**) or a block quote (**bq** or **ExtractPara**). Regardless of how they look in the current version of the manuscript, later on the designer is going to change the way they appear—so we can make small adjustments now to make them easier for us to work with.

There are two ways to do this, but before you make any tweaks, **save a copy** of the document for future reference. The copy acts as a backup in case things get out of hand, and it can act as a reference if you want to undo your formatting tweaks.

1. Edit a text style. To change a specific formatting aspect of a style, you can edit the style itself. If you use Word's direct-formatting menus, for example by clicking the $\boxed{I}$ button to revert an all-italics paragraph style to roman text to make it more legible, it will create an overlay on top of the style. Direct-formatting overlays have to be removed or replaced with text styles, so let's not add more of them. To edit a text style:

- In the Styles pane, hover over the name of the style you want to edit. Don't click on the style name, or you'll inadvertently apply the style to the paragraph or word where the cursor happens to be positioned in the manuscript. When you hover,  a small down-arrow, $\boxed{\vee}$, will appear to the right of the style-type label, as shown in the image.
- Click the arrow to reveal a menu, and select "Modify." The Modify Style window pops up.
- In the lower left of this window, click on the "Format" button. This brings up a list. The most useful options here are "Font" and "Paragraph."
- For example, Happenstance text styles have automatic

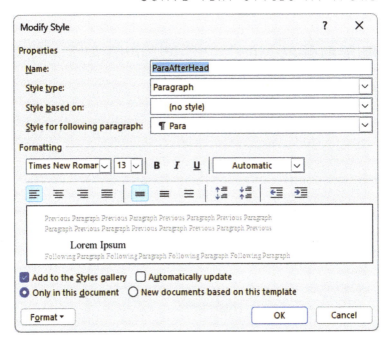

hyphenation turned on. Manuscript editors and copy-editors specifically find this difficult to work with—which hyphens were typed by the writer, and which have been automatically inserted by Word? The automatic hyphens won't carry over to the layout program, so it makes sense to get rid of them. To disable automatic hyphenation in the style:

- Select "Paragraph."
- In the Paragraph window, click on the top tab labeled "Line and page breaks."
- Check the box for "Don't hyphenate."
- As another example, some text style templates include headings in small caps. Editors specifically want to see what the text actually looks like without

any distracting decoration. To disable all-small-caps in a heading style:

- In the "Format" list of the Modify Style window, select "Font."
- In the Font window, click on the top tab labeled "Font."
- Uncheck the box for "Small caps."

2. Edit the text directly. The second way to tweak a text style is to edit the text directly, then redefine the text style. To use this method, the text you're formatting must already be formatted with the intended text style.

- Select the words or the paragraph you want to reformat.
- Using Word's "Font" or "Paragraph" ribbons, apply or remove formatting from the text. Examples: select one of the chapter headings, styled as **Chapter_Title**, and make the text red. In the manuscript the **Head_3** headings are italicized—select one of them and click Word's I button to remove the italics.
- In the Styles pane, there should be new entries in the list of styles that show the direct-formatting overlays. Using the examples above, "Chapter_Title + Red" shows that you formatted one or more instances of **Chapter_Title** in red, and "Head_3 + Not Italic" means you removed italics from one of the **Head_3** headings.
- If the overlays are not visible in the list, you can prompt the Styles pane to reassess which styles and overlays are in use in the document by clicking on the "Options" button at the bottom of the pane. In the Style Pane Options window, make sure all three boxes are checked under "Select formatting to show as styles," then click "OK."
- Hover over the base style

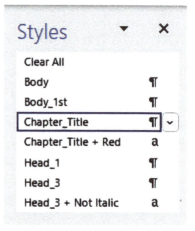

that's higher up the list, not the overlay, in these examples **Chapter_Title** or **Head_3**.

- A small down-arrow, ⌄ , will appear to the right of the style-type label.
- Click the arrow to reveal a menu, and select "Update Chapter_Title to match selection."
- The formatting changes you made are now part of the text style. Any text that is assigned this text style will update to look the same—all the chapter titles styled as **Chapter_Title** will be red.

You might want to make other changes in this way, for example if a font is hard to read, or the type is too large or too small, or even if you want all the chapter titles to be in a color so that they stand out when you're going through the manuscript.

Once you've completed work on a manuscript, you might want to undo the tweaks you've made and reset the text styles before you pass it on. The rationale for this, and a simple way to do it all at once, is explained below in "Keeping a repository or backup" (page 26).

Examples of tweaks for legibility

The two Word screen grabs below show the same set of styles. In the second image, some formatting details of the text styles have been tweaked to make it easier to read and easier to edit the manuscript.

In the first image, showing the original text styles I was provided with, I found the borders under the headings to be distracting. The fact that every level of heading is the same point size also makes it harder to make sense of the manuscript's content.

These issues have been corrected in the second image, along with removing the small caps from **Head_2**, removing the italics from **Head_3**, and using a more legible font for the body paragraphs. Adding color to each level of heading makes the document structure clearer for an editor scanning through the manuscript.

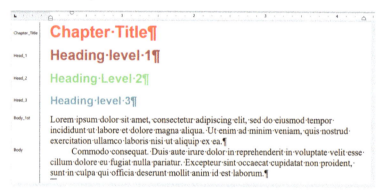

If you need to return the manuscript to your editor or designer without the colorful revisions, it's easy to restore the original formatting details after you've finished with the document. See "Reset the revised styles" below (page 29).

Keeping a repository or backup

If you make a lot of small tweaks to individual formatting elements of a set of text styles, as described above in "3. Tweak the text styles to make them more editing-friendly" (page 21), you might want to reset them all before you return the manuscript to your editor or client. A company that believes their system of text styles is flawless and intuitive and simple to work with might not be happy to see them revised, or worse, it might cause confusion farther down the line. Even though you're using the correct style name for each level of heading, if the color and point size are different, for example, at a cursory glance someone might assume you've used a different text style. The solution is to restore the original formatting elements to the document's text styles. This can be done for all the text styles at once in a simple operation.

Similar to importing text styles into the manuscript, described above in "1. Import the text styles" (page 14), you can reimport the original text styles into your completed manuscript. The look of the text will change, undoing all your tweaks, but nothing about the text itself will change, and the names of the text styles won't change. You also don't have to say good-bye to your improved styles—why not save them for future use? All this can be achieved in two steps:

1. **Export your revised styles** from the manuscript into a repository document for future use.
2. **Reset the revised styles** in the manuscript by replacing them with the original styles from an earlier version of the manuscript.

Export revised styles to use again later

Any Word document can serve as a repository for text styles. First, the process to save your tweaked styles:

- In Word, create a new document and save it with a name like repository for revised text styles.docx.
- Close the new document.
- Back in the manuscript, at the bottom of the Styles pane, click on "Manage Styles": the button is a capital A with a green checkmark on it, A.
- The Manage Styles window will pop up. At the bottom left of this window, click on "Import/Export." A window called "Organizer" will pop up.

In the Organizer window, the pane at left shows all the styles in the manuscript you're working on—including your tweaked styles. The pane at right shows all the styles in an external document, at first probably Word's built-in global template, called "Normal.dotm."

- On the Organizer's right pane, click on "Close File." The "Normal" list will close, and the button will change to "Open File."
- Click on "Open File." An Open window will pop up.
- At the bottom right of this Open window, click on the box that says "All Word templates." This will bring up a list of file types.
- Choose the "All Files" option, the first in the list.
- This Open window shows your local files. Locate the document you just created, repository for revised text styles .docx.
- Select the file and click "Open."

The right pane in the Organizer will now show all the text styles that are already contained in your repository document, likely just Word's default text styles. (When you create a new Word document, it automatically includes the default styles from Word's "Normal.dotx" template.)

- In the left pane, the manuscript with the tweaked styles, select the first style in the list by clicking on it; it will now be highlighted.
- Scroll to the bottom of the list of styles, then hold the SHIFT key, and click on the last style. The entire list will now be selected and highlighted.
- Between the two panes, click on the button labeled "Copy - >." This will copy all the text styles from the manuscript into the document on the right side—your styles repository.
- If a question box pops up to ask "Do you wish to overwrite existing style entries?" Just click "Yes."
- Close the Organizer window.

The next time you work on a similar manuscript from the same client, you can quickly import your tweaked text styles from your repository document using Word's Import/Export functions for text styles.

Reset the revised styles

Next, we want to replace the tweaked styles in the manuscript with the styles it started out with.

- In the manuscript, at the bottom of the Styles pane, click on "Manage Styles": the button is a capital A with a green checkmark on it, A.
- The Manage Styles window will pop up. At the bottom left of this window, click on "Import/Export." The "Organizer" window will pop up.

In the Organizer window, the pane at left shows all the styles in the manuscript you're working on. The pane at right shows all the styles in an external document, probably Word's built-in global template, called "Normal.dotm."

- On the Organizer's right pane, click on "Close File." The right-side list will disappear and the button will then change to "Open File."
- Click on "Open File." An Open window will pop up.
- At the bottom right of this Open window, click on the box that says "All Word templates." This will bring up a list of file types.
- Choose the "All Files" option, the first in the list.
- This Open window shows your local files. Locate the version of the manuscript you made as a backup, saved before you made any style tweaks.
- Select the file and click "Open."

The right pane in the Organizer will now show all the text styles that are contained in that older version of the manuscript. The list of styles will be the same as in the left pane.

- In the right pane, select the first style in the list by clicking on it; it will now be highlighted.
- Scroll to the bottom of the list of styles, then hold the SHIFT key, and click on the last style. The entire list will now be selected and highlighted.
- Between the two panels, click on the button labeled "< - Copy." This will copy all the text styles from the

older version of the manuscript into the document on the left side—the current version of the manuscript.

- A question box will pop up to ask "Do you wish to over-write existing style entries?" Just click "Yes." Nothing in the content of the text will change, and the style names won't change, but any formatting elements of the text styles that you tweaked will revert to their original form.
- Close the Organizer window.

Your tweaks to the text styles have now been overwritten, and you can pass the manuscript along to an editor or design-er without adding any confusion. Best of all, your tweaks are stored in that repository for you to use next time.

Formatting a manuscript with text styles

The best way to get familiar with the text styles in a specif-ic system is to look through the documentation. There are hundreds of styles in each of the systems, but don't get over-whelmed. Unless you're working on a complicated manu-script, it's likely that you'll be using only a few text styles, and most of the manuscript will be formatted with just a handful of basic text styles.

Below is a brief rundown:

Some commonly used text styles

meaning	in ScML	in Happen-stance	Word built-in styles
paragraph text styles			
a basic paragraph, or a basic indented paragraph	p	Para	Normal
the first paragraph of a chapter	pf	ParaAfterHead	Normal
the first paragraph after a subheading or a title	paft	ParaAfterHead	Normal

the continuation of a paragraph after a break in the text: after a block quote, a list, or a poem	pcon	ParaContinued	Normal

heading styles

the title of a chapter	ct	ChapterTitle	Heading 1
a first-level subheading within a chapter	ah	H1	Heading 2
a second-level subheading within a chapter	bh	H2	Heading 3

block quotes and extracts

a single-paragraph block quote	bqo	ExtractPara	Block Text
the first paragraph in a multiple-paragraph block quote	bqf	ExtractPara	Block Text
a subsequent paragraph in a block quote	bq	ExtractParaContinued	Block Text

basic character styles

italicized text	i	Italic	Italic
boldface text	b	Bold	Bold
text in small caps	sm	–	–
superscript characters	sup	Superscript	–

sidebars

heading in a sidebar	sbh	FeatureH1	–
regular paragraph in a sidebar	sb	FeaturePara	–
entry in a bulleted list in a sidebar	sbb1	FeatureListBulleted	–

frontmatter and backmatter styles

a chapter title or section title in the frontmatter: for a preface, introduction, table of contents	ctfm	ChapterTitle-Frontmatter	Heading 1
a chapter title or section title in the backmatter: an index, glossary, appendixes	ctbm	ChapterTitle-Backmatter	Heading 1

the dedication in a book	ded	Dedication	Normal *or* Emphasis
an epigraph	ep	Epigraph	Block Text
an entry in the index	in	Index I	Index I
an entry in the glossary	gt	GlossaryTerm	List
source citations and references			
a number or character that refers to a footnote	fnref	FootnoteReference	Footnote Reference
the text of a footnote	fn	Footnote	Footnote Text
a number or character that refers to an endnote	enref	EndnoteReference	Endnote Reference
the text of an endnote	en	Endnote	Endnote Text

The wrong way to show intention

The named text style itself is all the designer needs in order to know what to do with each part of the text. A paragraph that is styled as a regular paragraph, with **p** or **Para** or **Body**, doesn't need a bunch of spaces or a tab character at the beginning to show that it's indented. The designer will indent the text using the design software's capabilities, not using spaces. Typing five spaces or a tab at the start of a paragraph actually increases confusion: the regular paragraphs in some finished books or documents aren't indented but rather are set off by line space above and below. If you, as the content creator, want to have a say in the look of the final version, communicate with the designer. Don't try to show a preferred look by adding noise to the manuscript.

Similarly, a subheading within a chapter, styled as **ah** or **Head1**, doesn't need empty carriage returns above or below. From the name of the text style, the designer can see that it is intended to be a heading, and they will set up appropriate spacing around the headings using the design program. Extra carriage returns are just noise.

If you've inserted a quotation that should be indented,

don't use the spacebar or the tab key to do the indenting. Give the paragraph the correct style, **bqo** or **Block Quote** or **ExtractPara**, and the designer will make it look perfect.

Let the text styles do the talking for you. It's a hard habit for some writers to break, but adding meaningless characters only creates additional work for your editor or your designer. Your role is creating the content, not deciding how it should look. Free your mind, let it go, and let your designer handle that part of it.

When you've applied text styles, there is no need to type:

- empty carriage returns
- extra line space using a carriage return
- double spaces between sentences
- spaces or tabs to indent text

New text styles

One thing we shouldn't do is create new text styles, unless you're creating your own universe and not working with an existing system of styles. The people who built ScML and Happenstance, among other text style systems, have thought through all the possible needs we might have. Look through the documentation for these systems to find the text style that already exists for the intention you have. It's extremely unlikely you'll need to create a new text style for a situation no one has encountered before. If your editor provided you with a set of text styles, they will want you to shoehorn that slightly square peg into the rounded hole of an existing text style rather than create a new one.

How granular should styles be?

The brief sampling of text styles above (page 30) demonstrates the limitations of Word's built-in text styles: They don't differentiate between a paragraph that appears after a heading and a subsequent regular paragraph, for example, and chapter titles and chapter subheadings are handled with the same **Heading** styles. ScML is a highly granular system, and differentiates between **paft**, the first paragraph after a heading, and **pf**, the first paragraph after a chapter title. In the iteration of the Happenstance collection that I've seen, no distinction is made between these two, and both would be styled as **ParaAfterHead**. In the Happenstance system a sidebar is marked **FeatureH1**, while in ScML the style **sbh** is used for the heading of individual sidebars and **sbt** is used for repeating sidebar headings.

ScML has a level of granularity that you might not ever need. For numbered lists, for example, the basic style in **nl**, but there's also **nlf**, for the first entry in a numbered list, and **nll**, the last entry in a numbered list. This granularity can be useful in the design stage, for example if the designer wants to add consistent line space above and below the whole list but not between lines in the list. Check with your designer or your editor as to whether you should implement first and last styles or just make the whole list **nl**.

How to apply text styles

In Word, there are two ways to apply text styles to paragraphs or parts of paragraphs:

1. Apply styles from the Styles pane. If you don't have the Styles pane open, you can summon it with the keyboard shortcut CTRL+SHIFT+ALT+S (hold down the CTRL, ALT, and SHIFT keys at the same time, and type s).

- Select the paragraph or the words you want to format. To apply a character style, select all the specific words. To apply a paragraph style, you can select the whole paragraph, but it usually works just to position the cursor somewhere in the paragraph. You can select multiple paragraphs at once to apply the same style.
- In the Styles pane on the right, find the name of the style you want to apply and click on it.

  For a paragraph style, the paragraph should shift to this formatting, and the label in the Style area pane on the left side (explained on page 19) should change to the new style's name. The Styles pane on the right will show the paragraph style highlighted, with a border around it.

For a character style, the words should shift to that formatting. Character styles aren't shown in the Style area pane on the left, where only the underlying paragraph style is displayed, but the Styles pane on the right will show the character style highlighted, with a border around it.

2. Apply styles from the Apply Styles pop-up. This little pop-up box is summoned with a keyboard shortcut: CTRL+SHIFT+S (hold down the CTRL and SHIFT keys at the same time, and type s). This method works best once you're familiar with the text style names and know which one you want without consulting the list.

- Select the paragraph or the words you want to format. To apply a character style, select all the specific words. To apply a paragraph style, you can select the whole paragraph, but it usually works just to position the cursor somewhere in the paragraph. You can select multiple paragraphs at once to apply the same style.
- In the Apply Styles box, type the style name. It will autocomplete the name for you, so if you type "p" it might fill in "paft" or "pcon" or "Para." Hit Enter to accept it and apply the style shown, or backspace over the letters if you want only "p."

Working with combined styles

Combined text styles, also called linked styles, marked by ¶a in the Styles pane, have both paragraph and character formatting. If you apply the style to an entire paragraph in Word, including the pilcrow ¶ that marks the end of the paragraph, the paragraph style is applied. If you apply the style to individual words, the character formatting of the style is applied without impacting the underlying paragraph. In Word the style is listed as a single entry in the Styles pane, but when the manuscript is imported into InDesign, it is split into separate paragraph and character styles.

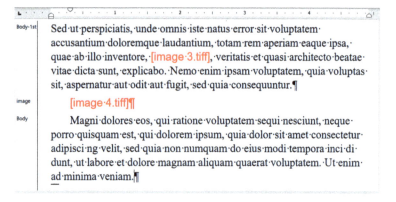

An example of a useful combined style is **image**, illustrated in the Word screenshot above. **image** is intended to mark in the manuscript the names of graphics that will be placed later, in the design phase. If it's applied to a whole paragraph, the paragraph formatting includes some line space above and below, as in the second paragraph. If it's applied to individual words, the same character formatting—the red character color—makes it stand out. **image** is thus useful to identify two kinds of images: inline images within the text, like "[image 3.tiff]," and images that are placed outside paragraphs, like "[image 4.tiff]." During the design process, the designer can quickly scan the manuscript and find the tags for all the images.

Cleaning up the style overlays

First, make sure you can see all the overlays. In the Styles pane:

- At the bottom of the Styles pane, click on the button labeled "Options." The Style Pane Options window pops up.

- In "Select styles to show," choose "In use." For this task we don't need to see all the styles that are available, only the ones that are currently used in the document.

- In "Select how list is sorted," it should be set to "Alphabetical."

- Under "Select formatting to show as styles," check all three checkboxes. When these boxes are checked, the list of styles in the Styles pane includes all the direct-formatting overlays.

- Click "OK."

Direct-formatting overlays persist

Note that if the text has direct formatting applied to it, this will remain as character overlays even when you've changed the paragraph style. For example, if the writer formatted one sentence in a paragraph with green text, and you applied the **Para** or **p** style to the paragraph, the green-text direct formatting is still there.

Direct-formatting overlays appear in the Styles pane list with a plus sign. If the writer has added color to a regular paragraph, for example, the list in the Styles pane will include the style "p" or "Para" as well as a separate entry "p + Green" or "Para + Green." The plus sign indicates that "Green" is a direct-formatting overlay, not a style.

Another example: the writer or another contributor changed some or all of the words in a heading to a larger point size. When you first got the manuscript, the styles list would have included something like "Heading 1"

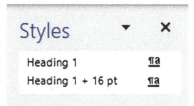

(one of Word's built-in default styles) as well as an entry for "Heading 1 + 16 pt." The "16 pt" is somebody's direct formatting, an overlay of the paragraph style. After you applied the ScML **ah** style to this heading, for example, the styles list will include "ah" as well as "ah + 16 pt." The paragraph style is now the one you want, but the direct-formatting overlay persists.

Meaningful versus meaningless overlays

Depending on how much direct formatting is in the manuscript, there might be a lot of these overlays. Sometimes they are combined in a lengthy list in the Styles pane, like "Normal + 16pt, Green, Condensed by 0.5 pt, Before: 6 pt." Some overlays may be meaningless, like adding a different font to the chapter titles and headings. Some overlays might be informative to an editor when they are confirming the writer's intent and applying text styles, like when a writer consistently puts all the A-level heads in 18-point type and all the B-level heads in 14-point type, or perhaps puts all the block quotes in blue text, "Normal + Blue." Once these headings have the styles **ah** and **bh** applied, however, and the block quotes have been marked as **bq**, the point size and the blue text become meaningless.

Other overlays are meaningful, and they need to be converted to character styles. Most notably this is about boldface and italics. **Read through the list in the Styles pane to determine which overlays might be meaningful.**

Convert an overlay to a character style

In the example of the Styles pane below, the style **p** has two direct-formatting overlays, boldface and italics. As the writer or the editor reviewing the manuscript, you've decided both italics and boldface need to be retained in the project. You don't have go through the text line by line to apply these character styles to each instance. The simplest way to retain this formatting is to do it all at once, by converting the direct formatting to character styles:

- In the Styles pane, hover over the style with the overlay, in this example "p + Bold." Don't click on the name, or you'll inadvertently apply the style to the paragraph or word where the cursor happens to be positioned in the manuscript.

- Click on the down-arrow that appears at the right. This brings up a menu.

- Choose "Select all instances." In a large document, this selection process can take some time, even several minutes; be patient! Word will show you a progress bar in the lower right of the main window. Once all the instances are selected, you'll see one or more of them highlighted in the manuscript.

- Apply the text style for boldface, in the ScML system named **b**, by either clicking on "b" in the Styles pane list, or by typing "b" in the Apply Styles box (see "How to apply text styles," page 34).

- It may take a minute for everything to reformat, but eventually the list of styles in the Styles pane will change. The "p + Bold" item should disappear, and if it wasn't there before, the character style "b" will be added to the list.

- You can prompt the Styles pane to reassess which styles and overlays are in use in the document by clicking on the "Options" button at the bottom of the pane, then in the Style Options window, click "OK."

- If "p + Bold" persists in the list (this happens sometimes for reasons unknown), you can double-check that the overlay really is gone by hovering over it and clicking the down-arrow again. Instead of an option to "Select all instances," the menu should say "Not currently used."

- Use the same process to replace the italics overlay: select all the instances of "p + Italic," then apply the character style for italics, in ScML named **i**.

This select-and-replace capability can be a huge time-saver. With just a few steps, you've applied a style throughout the document. As an editor working on a lengthy manuscript, if the writer has used consistent direct formatting, you might also be able to save yourself some drudgery with this procedure. For example, if the writer has formatted all the chapter titles in 20-point boldface type, you can select all the instances of "Heading 1 + 20 pt + Bold" and apply the paragraph style for chapter titles, in ScML named **ct**.

Remove a superfluous overlay

To remove meaningless direct formatting like added fonts, added text colors, or altered point sizes, the procedure is similar. In the example of the Styles pane below, we can see that one or more instances of the **H1** paragraph style have an unnecessary overlay with a font. To remove the superfluous overlays:

- In the Styles pane, hover over the style with the overlay, in this example "H1 + Comic Sans MS." Don't click on the name, or you'll inadvertently apply the style to the paragraph or word where the cursor happens to be positioned in the manuscript.
- Click on the down-arrow ⌄ that appears at the right. This brings up a menu.
- Choose "Select all instances." In a large document, this selection process can take some time,

Styles ▾ ✕

H1	¶
H1 + Comic Sans MS	a ⌄
H2	¶
H3	¶
Italic	a
LinkURL	a
ListBulleted	¶
Normal	¶
Para	¶
ParaAfterHead	¶
ParaAfterHead + 16 pt	a
ParaContinued	¶

even several minutes; be patient! Word will show you a progress bar in the lower right of the main window. Once all the instances are selected, you'll see one or more of them highlighted in the manuscript.
- Click on the Clear All Formatting button, A◇. It is found on Word's Home tab in the Font area. You can get the same result more easily by typing CTRL+SPACEBAR (hold down the CTRL key and type a space).
- It may take a minute for everything to reformat, but eventually the list of styles in the Styles pane will change. The "H1 + Comic Sans MS" item should disappear.
- You can prompt the Styles pane to reassess which styles and overlays are in use in the document by clicking on the "Options" button at the bottom of the pane, then in the Style Options window, just click "OK."
- If "H1 + Comic Sans MS" persists in the list (this happens sometimes for reasons unknown), you can double-check that the overlay really is gone by hovering over it and clicking the down-arrow again. Instead of an option to "Select all instances," the menu should say "Not currently used."

The work of removing spurious overlays can be arduous in a lengthy manuscript. If there is a lot of direct formatting, there can be dozens of these entries in the styles list. Often the most efficient approach is a combination of revising styles in the Styles pane and applying text styles directly to sections of the manuscript where the intent is evident, regardless of how they're formatted.

Bulk removal of superfluous overlays

It's possible to remove all the overlays that apply to a specific style with one click. The risk to this procedure is that you might inadvertently remove a meaningful overlay along with the superfluous ones. Along with the unnecessary font overlay you might remove some crucial italics, for example. Look through the list of overlays carefully before you do this to make sure none of the overlays are formatting that need to be retained.

Another reason not to bulk-remove all the formatting overlays is that you might lose information that can help you determine the intent of different paragraphs. It's important for editors to go through a manuscript with this in mind: Does any of the direct formatting show the writer's intent?

A writer will typically compose a manuscript without considering text styles, rendering the entire document in Word's **Normal** style. These writers differentiate the chapter titles by adding direct formatting, for example to center the chapter title and make it larger. In the Styles pane this would appear as "Normal + 16 pt + Center." Once you've determined that these specific overlays are for chapter titles, it makes sense to convert them all to the correct paragraph style, like **ct** or **ChapterTitle**. Unfortunately many writers don't apply direct formatting consistently. Sometimes a chapter title will be formatted as 16 points, and sometimes 18 points. Instead of centering the chapter titles, some of them might be aligned with a series of tabs.

In the example Styles pane, the paragraph style **Body** has several overlays. In this project, the font, color, and point size overlays are not important, but the italics need to be retained. In brief, the easiest way to reduce all the overlays to just the paragraph style **Body** and the character style **Ital**:

- Select all the instances of **Body** with an italics overlay and apply the character style **Ital**.
- Select all remaining instances of **Body** and apply the paragraph style **Body**. This removes all the remaining overlays.

The steps to removing the overlays in this example:

- In the Styles pane, note that there are two overlays that contain italic formatting, the first and last in the list.
- Convert both using "Convert an overlay to a character style," page 38.

The rest of the overlays to the Body text style still remain. If you're certain that all of them are superfluous, and none of them need to be retained, you can remove them all with one click:

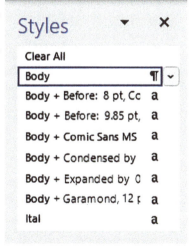

- Hover over the first **Body** entry in the list, the one that has no overlays. Don't click on the style name, or you'll inadvertently apply the style to the paragraph where the cursor happens to be positioned in the manuscript.
- Click on the down-arrow ⌄ that appears at the right. This brings up a menu.

- Choose "Select all instances." In a large document, this selection process can take some time, even several minutes; be patient! Word will show you a progress bar in the lower right of the main window. Once all the instances are selected, you'll see one or more of them highlighted in the manuscript.
- Click on the **Body** entry in the Styles pane list. This will revert all the instances that have overlays to the base **Body** style.

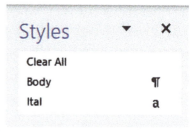

- It may take a minute for everything to reformat, but eventually the list of styles in the Styles pane will change. All the "Body +" overlays should disappear, leaving only **Body**.
- You can prompt the Styles pane to reassess which styles and overlays are in use in the document by clicking on the "Options" button at the bottom of the pane, then in the Style Options window, click "OK."

Indelible overlays

Some overlays can't be removed—specifically this involves certain **mathematical symbols** and **characters from other writing systems**. Roman, Greek, and Cyrillic characters seem to render normally in Word's paragraph styles, but Chinese characters, Hangul, and other writing systems are handled as font overlays. I suspect this might vary depending on what languages are installed in the computer's operating system and perhaps in Word.

Examples of these unalterable overlays in the Styles pane are "p + Cambria Math" or "Para + MS Mincho." Because they can't be altered, our choice is either to leave them as they are, or mark them with a character style that indicates "nonstandard char-

acters." The designer or project editor might have a pref-
erence. In ScML the
appropriate character style to
mark the characters as nonstandard is lang, and in Happenstance it's **Custom-
CharStyle**.

Removing direct formatting anywhere

Word's Clear All Formatting function, using the A̶ button or CTRL+SPACEBAR (hold down the CTRL key and type a
space), is a **powerful tool.** It does two things to any text that
you select in the document:

- **removes any direct formatting** and reverts the text to its
  essential paragraph style
- **removes any character styles** and reverts the text to only
  its paragraph style

When we write or edit a document using text styles, it's
necessary to shift our habits away from direct formatting.
When you encounter a word that should be italicized, for example, instead of clicking on the word processor's $\boxed{I}$ button
to apply an overlay, logically you would click on the character
style named Italic or Ital or i in the Styles pane. Similarly,
when you find a word that shouldn't be italicized, the best way
to remove the overlay is to select the word and remove the direct formatting: click the A̶ button or type CTRL+SPACEBAR.
If you simply click on the $\boxed{I}$ button, it might remove the
direct formatting, or it might introduce a new overlay: if the
text is already formatted with the Ital character style, for example, clicking the $\boxed{I}$ button will add a new overlay that will
appear in the Styles pane list as something nonsensical like
"Ital + Not Italic." Using the A̶ button or CTRL+SPACEBAR
avoids this possibility by removing both overlays and character styles—you don't even have to know how the text was
formatted, as it will be reset to its underlying paragraph style.

Moving Styles into InDesign

To transfer the text of a manuscript from the word processor file into the design layout, we use InDesign's Place function. The process is explained in detail below, but to summarize:

1. Import the text manuscript into your InDesign layout.
2. Remove any inadvertent text overrides.
3. Remove the formatting from any unintended character styles.

Text frames

Text imported into an InDesign layout can be placed either in the basic frame that exists on the pages, called the primary text frame, or into a singular text box. Using the default settings, placing it in the primary text frame will overwrite whatever text is already there. To append the text instead, see "Import Options" (page 48). Another way to retain any text that's already in the layout is to create a new box using the Rectangle Frame tool, ⊠, and place the text in the new box. The text can then be threaded to flow from this box into the primary text frame or into other text boxes.

Threading text is a fundamental and nuanced InDesign skill, but to summarize, you can make the text flow from one box or frame into another, or into the primary frame. Each text box or frame has an "out port" on the right edge near the bottom and an "in port" at the left edge near the top, shown in the image. With the Selection tool, 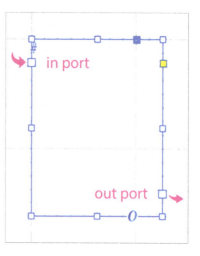, click on the out port of one box and then the in port of another—this creates a link between the boxes, and the text will flow from one to the next. But first, you have to import the text.

1. Import the text

To retain the text's formatting and text styles, text has to be imported into an InDesign document in a specific way. Copying text from a word processor document and then pasting it into the InDesign layout doesn't work—the text itself transfers, but you will lose all the formatting and text styles. The only way to import text intact, with all the formatting and text styles, is InDesign's **Place function**. The Place function works in one of two ways:

- Select the "File" menu, then "Place," and choose the file that contains the text manuscript. The InDesign keyboard shortcut for this is CTRL-D or ⌘-D.
- Alternately, drag the text manuscript file from File Explorer or Finder and drop it into the text frame or text box in the InDesign layout.

Import options

If you use the Place function instead of drag-and-drop, you can access options for the text import. In the Place dialog box, one of the options at the bottom is a checkbox to "**Replace Selected Item**." Unselecting this checkbox means you can place the text in the primary text frame without overwriting any existing text.

Also in the Place dialog box, one of the options at the bottom is a checkbox to "**Show Import Options**." The default settings usually work fine, but if you check this box, an options window appears as the next step, shown below. Because we want the text styles to come in along with the text, definitely don't select the option "Remove Styles and Formatting" in this options window—that is equivalent to cutting and pasting plain text.

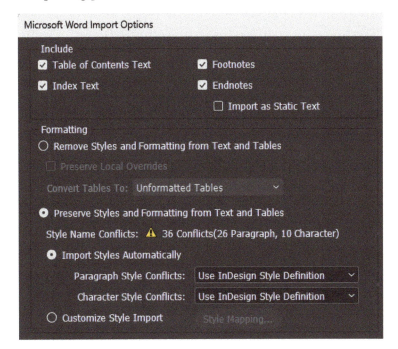

If there is already text in the document with text style names that overlap the incoming text, the Import Options box will show a warning: "Style Name Conflicts ⚠." The easiest path is to select "Import Styles Automatically" and make sure the boxes below it have "Use InDesign Style Definition" selected. This means the incoming text will retain all the style names, but the formatting for each style already in the document will use the existing InDesign version, not the formatting from the text document.

Style Mapping

In the Place Options window, the default is "Import Styles Automatically." If your InDesign layout already contains text styles that you're using, but the style names differ in the incoming text, you can link each of the incoming text file's text styles to an existing style in the InDesign document. Choose "Customize Style Import" and go through the **Style Mapping** list. Style Mapping can also be useful to deal with any styles coming in that aren't already in use in the InDesign layout.

If you don't bother with Style Mapping, the default is that InDesign will create new styles for any styles in the text document that don't exist in the InDesign layout. If a style has the same name, the default is to use the formatting settings of the text style that already exists in InDesign, overriding the incoming formatting of the text style.

Style Mapping can be useful when you're doing layout for a subsequent book in a series, or a newsletter that has the same layout as a previous edition. In both cases, if you have text styles already established in your InDesign layout, Style Mapping can simplify your work.

Imported text is not linked

When you place an image or graphic element in an InDesign document, the image appears in the document's list of links in the Links panel, accessed with the 🔗 button. When you revise a graphic somewhere else, like in a photo editing program, InDesign keeps track of that and updates it for you, or asks if you want to update the image. That doesn't happen when you place text. InDesign imports the text from the text file, but the text file won't appear in the Links panel. If the text file is revised after it's imported, InDesign doesn't know about it, and the text won't automatically update—it will have to be imported and placed again.

Hands off the text

The fact that InDesign doesn't incorporate updates to text files is actually a huge benefit to designers. The last thing you need is someone else revising part of the layout that you've already placed and adjusted. A fundamental tenet of the publishing work flow is that each stage of the process can be completed without interference from ahead or behind. If you're doing layout with the text, the text can't change until you're finished with it and pass it along for review or proofreading.

Here's the best way to conceptualize placing the text in your design: **The text that's in the layout is the one and only version of the manuscript.** Text shouldn't get imported into your layout until the writers and editors have finalized it. The writers and editors should clearly understand that they can't make any further edits to the text once it has been turned over to you. Once it has been imported and placed in your layout, the text is immutable until after the design work, when the final version gets proofread.

If a writer or editor tells you, "We might send some small text edits for you to make while you're working on the layout," you should firmly refuse: "Let's wait to start the layout work until the text is finalized." Trying to incorporate a stream of minor text revisions while you're working will add significantly to your work time. Explain to the content creators that they'll have the opportunity to make minor revisions in the proof-reading stage—but that the text should be finalized and letter-perfect before you take charge of it to do the layout.

If you allow those "few small tweaks" while you're working, they can easily snowball into major text revisions or hourly updates with "I found one more thing …" Trust me: if you don't hold firm to this boundary up front, you will feel the pain later.

The Styles panels

Once you've imported the text, the text styles appear in the Style panels, one for paragraph styles and one for character styles. If they're not already visible, these panels can be accessed by selecting the "Window" menu and then "Styles." If you drag the Paragraph Styles panel into the

vertical dock on the right side of InDesign's main window, the button for it is 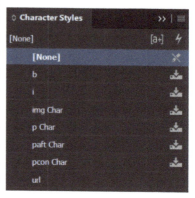. For character styles, and to summon the Character Styles panel, the button in the dock is █.

If the source text contained combined styles, the text import process may have split the style into a separate paragraph style and character style. In the Paragraph Styles panel the style will have the same name as it did in the word processor, and in the Character Styles panel it will be named with the original name plus "Char." The new character style will only appear if the style was applied to individual words in the manuscript. If it was only applied to whole paragraphs, it will only appear as a paragraph style. Combined styles are explained in detail above in "Working with combined styles," page 35.

The Styles panels are ground zero for working with text styles in InDesign. To apply a style to a section of text, just select the text with the Text tool, █, and click on the name of the style in the Styles panel. Much more about working with text styles in InDesign is in the next chapter.

Based-on styles

Once you've imported the text, the list of text styles in the Styles panels might include some unfamiliar ones—text styles that the writer or editor didn't use. If a text style that is used in the manuscript is based on another text style, the import process brings in both of them. An example in the ScML system is that all the *bl* text styles, used for bulleted lists, are based on the numbered list styles. So even if the manuscript doesn't use *nl*, *nlf*, and *nll*, they will be imported too if your document uses *bl*, *blf*, and *bll*.

Even though they're not being used directly, don't delete these styles from the list, as their basic formatting actually is in use—by other styles. This based-on linking is actually a superpower: if a subset of related paragraph styles, for example **pf**, **paft**, **pcon**, and **psec**, are based on the fundamental **p** text style, you can change the formatting of the **p** text style—things like the font, the point size, and the leading—and see it carried over to all the styles that are based on **p**. More about working with based-on styles, and how to disconnect the based-on links, appears in "Based-on styles" (page 67) in the next chapter.

2. Eliminate leftover direct formatting

Before you set to work adjusting text styles and copyfitting, the first thing to do with the new text is to clean up any inadvertently imported direct formatting. Ideally the incoming text is formatted only with paragraph styles and character styles and doesn't contain any direct formatting, but oftentimes some direct formatting inadvertently gets included. Some of this direct formatting may be lost during the import process, but in other instances, InDesign will mark direct formatting as an **override** of the text style.

It's a good practice is to get rid of all the unintended overrides up front. The process is simple:

- Select all the text: with the Text tool, 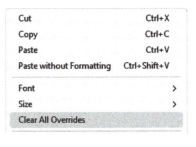, position the cursor somewhere in the text frame, then type CTRL-A or ⌘-A. All the text will be highlighted.
- Right-click on the text. In the menu that pops up, select **Clear All Overrides**. If there aren't any overrides, this option won't appear on the menu.

Cut	Ctrl+X
Copy	Ctrl+C
Paste	Ctrl+V
Paste without Formatting	Ctrl+Shift+V
Font	>
Size	>
Clear All Overrides	

To assess whether there are overrides on a specific part of the text, see "Text style overrides" (page 62) in the next chapter.

3. Remove inadvertent character styles

In a complex manuscript, spurious or undesired character styles can be imported with the text. Most often these are split from combined styles (explained in "Working with combined styles," page 35) and appear in the Character Styles panel, often with "Char" at the end of the name. These styles can override your design if they bring character formatting with them.

An example is if the writer or editor used a character style to mark words in the manuscript as terms that should go in the book's glossary or in an index. Character styles for this purpose in the ScML system have names like **gtref** and **idx**. The character style brings with it whatever font was in use in the word processor, in Microsoft Word typically Times New Roman or Calibri, and possibly a different character color or point size. The design of the document doesn't need these terms to be highlighted, so you either have to remove the character style or reset its formatting. Often the character style needs to remain intact for someone else in the production process, for example the person who is preparing the index. If you're unsure, don't remove the character style, just remove all its formatting:

- Pull up the Character Styles panel, accessed from InDesign's "Window" menu or the ⊡A dock button.
- Right-click on the name of the problematic style, and from the menu that appears, select "Edit."
- The Character Style Options window appears, shown below.
- The style's formatting elements are listed in the Style Settings box, and you can go through the list of attributes on the left side to see them individually. Under "Basic Character Formats," for example, you'll likely find the straggler font from the word processor, and the unexpected color is under "Character Color."
- There's no need to adjust these formatting attributes individually—you can remove all of them at once.

- If you do want to retain some of the formatting attributes, for example a different color or font weight for text marked as a URL, see "Creating a new character style" (page 64) in the next chapter.
- On the left side of the Character Style Options window, click on the top item, "General." On the right side of the window, click "Reset to Base." This removes all the style's formatting. The Style Settings box will revert to simply "[None]."

You have effectively made the style invisible: text marked with this character style won't look any different from the underlying paragraph it's in. But if the character style is needed later, it's still in the document.

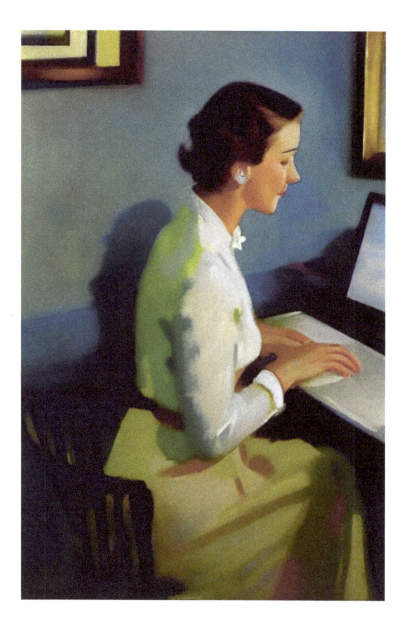

Using Styles in InDesign

Using text styles speeds up design and layout. Instead of guessing what the section headings or pull quotes are supposed to be, the writer or editor's intent is clearly marked with a text style. Any revision you make to a text style applies that formatting to all instances of that style. Instead of tweaking the color of every section heading or the point size of each image caption, you only have to change it once.

Adjusting the design by revising text styles

It might be tempting to go through a layout and adjust individual paragraphs and other elements to get the look you want. But to maintain consistency through the document, you can make an adjustment just once when you revise the text style, instead of adjusting the text itself. There are two ways to edit the formatting contained in a text style and apply it to all the instances of that style:

1. **Revise one instance** in the document. When it looks the way you want, redefine the text style with these new parameters. The new formatting will be applied to all instances of the text style.
2. Edit the text style in the **Paragraph Style Options window** with the Preview checkbox selected. As you make adjustments, the layout will change in real time.

Revise one instance

When you change the formatting of a paragraph or a section of text, you are applying **overrides**. The override formatting only applies to the text you're working on. But once you get the look you want, place the cursor in the text with the revised formatting and open the Paragraph Styles panel. The paragraph style of the paragraph is highlighted, and a plus sign appears after its name. The plus sign means there is an override to the style—something has been added.

An example: You want the second-level headings to be a little larger, and to be in dark red.

- Select the text of one of these headings with the Text tool, 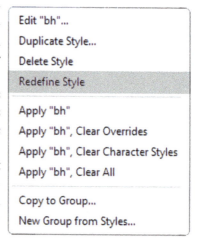.

- Use the Properties panel to increase the point size, and the Color panel to apply the character color you want. In the Paragraph Styles panel, accessed from the "Window" menu or the 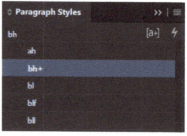 dock button, the second-level heads will bear a style name like **H2** or **B-head**, or in this example from the ScML collection, **bh**. Because you've added overrides—the larger point size and the new character color—the name appears with the plus sign as "bh+" (or "H2+" or "B-head+").

- To apply your revisions to all instances of this style, right-click on the style name.

- From the menu that comes up, select "Redefine Style." The plus sign goes away, and in the layout all instances of the text style are now formatted with your revisions. You've turned your overrides into the text style.

Some overrides, like italics and boldface, apply only to some words or characters and not to the whole paragraph. Redefining the paragraph style will apply the overrides to the whole paragraph. For these character overrides, you can create a new character style—see "Create a completely new character style" below (page 66).

The Paragraph Style Options window

- In the Paragraph Styles panel, right-click on the text style name that you want to tweak the formatting for.
- From the menu that comes up, select "Edit." The Paragraph Style Options window appears, shown below.
- In the lower left, check the box for "Preview." As you revise the formatting in the Paragraph Style Options window, the layout will update in real time.

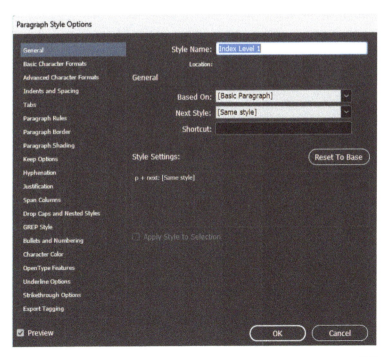

- On the left side of the box, a list of all the formatting categories appears. You can adjust formatting basics for the whole paragraph, like the font and the point size, how the paragraph is justified, hyphenation, character color, even background shading. For heading text styles, you can specify that they always appear at the top of the next column, or on the next recto page.

- Once you've revised the formatting of a text style, the ![icon] icon disappears from the text style's entry in the Styles panel.

More universal character styles

Sometimes the incoming text styles will include formatting elements that you don't want. For a paragraph style, you can easily change the formatting, as explained above. Some character styles need to have a formatting element removed completely rather than just being revised. An example is a character style for italics. In the word processor, every paragraph might have been formatted with the font Times New Roman. When the character style for italics, *i* or **Ital** or **Italic**, is imported into InDesign, it might include Times New Roman as one of its formats. In your layout, none of the fonts used is Times New Roman—ideally the *i* or **Ital** character style will use the italicized form of any font it is applied to. The remedy is to make the character style more universal by removing the specified font, or a specified point size, or any other formatting element, leaving just the basic "Italic" font style.

- First, pull up the Character Style Options window: In the Character Styles panel, right-click on the name of the style, and from the menu select "Edit." The Character Style Options window appears, shown below.

- The Style Settings box shows a list of the formatting elements. In this example, for the **Ital** character style, the font is set to Times New Roman, shown by "+ Times New Roman" and the font style is set to italics, shown by "+ Italic." On the left side, you can click on "Basic Character Formats" to see the same thing, that the Font

Style is "Italics" and the base font is specified in the Font Family box. Clicking this box allows you to choose a different font, but we want to remove it altogether.

- On the left side of the Character Style Options window, click on "General." On the right side, click "Reset to Base" to remove all the formatting. This will remove the base font, but it also removes everything else, including the italics format.

- You have to go back into "Basic Character Formats" in the list at left, and in the Font Style box, select "Italic."

One complication is that not every font has a style called "Italic." You might have to create different italicizing character styles for different fonts in the layout: **i-p** for the body text to apply to **p**, **pf**, **paft**, and **pcon** paragraph styles, and **i-headings** to apply to elements that use a different font, like chapter titles and subheadings **ct**, **ah**, and **bh**. But the extra work of creating more than one italicizing character style is still preferable to having all your italics rendered in a straggler font from the word processor.

Using a character style for boldface, like **b** or **bf** or **Bold**, is even more complicated: most fonts for printed materials have several different weights rather than a simple "Bold" style. You might have to create a new boldface character style for each font, but the advantage is that the layout will look exactly the way you want it to. See "Create a completely new character style" (page 66).

Text style overrides

It's easy to tell if there's an override on any part of the text. Using the Text tool, **T**, position the cursor in the text, or select part of the text. In the Style panel, the name of the text style will be highlighted. If there are any overrides, a plus sign appears after the style name. If the style name appears as "p+" or "bh+" or "ct+" it means some formatting has been added.

Apply text styles

To apply a style to a section of text, select the text with the Text tool, **T**. Open the Styles panel, either for paragraph styles ⊞ or character styles ⊞, and click on the name of the style.

Creating a new paragraph style

To fine-tune the layout, sometimes it's necessary to create more granular text styles. An example might be that the sub-headings require less line spacing above them when they follow a table or an image than when they follow a block of text. If the imported text has all the subheadings styled as **ah**, you can easily create a new text style based on it that has the new line spacing. There are two ways to create a new style based on an existing one:

Duplicate Style

- In the Paragraph Styles panel, right-click on the style, in this example **ah**.
- From the menu, select "Duplicate Style." The Duplicate Paragraph Style window, similar to the Paragraph Style Op-

Edit "ah"...
Duplicate Style...
Delete Style
Apply "ah"
Copy to Group...
New Group from Styles...

tions window, will appear for the new style. The default name of the new style is "ah copy," but you can give it a more logical name. If you want to use it for all the sub-headings that follow an image, for example, name the new style something like **ah-after-image** or **ah-image**.

- In the "Based On" window, choose **ah**. That way, if you change the font or the character color or any other formatting for your subheadings, the new style will change too. The only formatting that won't change is what you add to this new style.

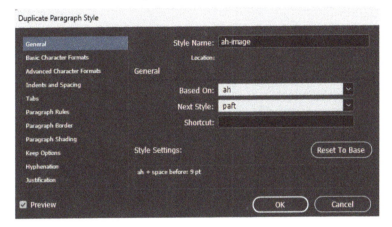

- You can change any of the formatting elements for this new style. Using the example above, that you need headings with less line spacing, in the Duplicate Paragraph Style window, select "Indents and Spacing" from the list at left and make the adjustment.

The adjustments you've made are shown in the Style Settings box. For the new **ah-image** style, "+ space before: 9 pt" is what differs from the **ah** style it's based on. The differences listed in the Style Settings box are the only elements that won't automatically update for **ah-image** when you revise **ah**.

Revise one instance

- With the Text tool, , select the instance of the text style that you want to change. Using the same example, about creating another version of the **ah** style with different spacing, look to the Paragraph Styles panel to see that **ah** is highlighted.

- Open the Paragraph window, either in the Properties dock, or from the Type menu and choose "Paragraph." Once you've changed the spacing, in the Paragraph Styles panel the style name will appear with a plus sign, "ah+." The plus sign means the style has something added—an override.

- At the bottom of the Paragraph Styles panel, click on the Create New Style button, 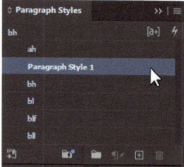. This will add to the list a new style, named **Paragraph Style 1**, that contains all the formatting of **ah** plus the override you made.

- Right-click on this new style to bring up the Paragraph Style Options window, where you can rename it with something more logical, like **ah-after-image** or **ah-image**. The "Based On" window should show that its parent is **ah**, and any revisions you make to **ah** will be reflected in **ah-image**—except the overrides you made, in this example regarding line spacing.

Creating a new character style

The same process can be used to create new character styles. An example: in addition to basic boldface text, you want some instances of boldface to be in blue. Three ways to create a new character style:

Duplicate an existing character style

- In the Character Styles panel, right-click on the style, in this example the style for boldface, **b**.

- From the menu, select "Duplicate Style." The Duplicate Character Style window, similar to the Character Style Options window, will appear for the new style. The default name of the new style is "b copy," but you can give it a more logical name. If you want blue boldface, for example, name the new style something like **b-blue**.

- In the "Based On" window, you can choose **b** to keep the new style linked to the original. If the character style only includes the font weight and the character color, linking them is probably not necessary. If the **b** and **b-blue** styles also include a different font or some other formatting element, linking them is useful to maintain consistency with any changes you might make to **b**.

- You can change any of the formatting elements for this new style. Using the example above, that you need a boldface style in blue, select "Character Color" from the list at left in the Duplicate Character Style window and apply the new color. If that's the only formatting that you change for **b-blue**, it's also the only thing that won't update when you revise the style it's based on, **b**.

Revise one instance

- With the Text tool, **T**, select the words that you want to change. Using the same example, about creating a blue version of **b**, the words you select will already have **b** applied.

- Look to the Character Styles panel to see that **b** is highlighted. If the words didn't already have a text style applied to them, "[None]" will be highlighted. That means you're creating a new character style from scratch—jump to the next section, "Create a completely new character style" (page 66).

- Open the Color window, either from the dock on the right, or from the Window menu, and choose "Color." Once you've changed the character color, in the Character Styles panel, the style name will appear with a plus sign, "b+." The plus sign means the style has something added—an override.

- At the bottom of the Character Styles panel, click on the Create New Style button, ⊞. This will add to the list a new style, named **Character Style 1**, that contains all the formatting of **b** plus the override you made.
- Right-click on this new style to bring up the Character Style Options window, where you can rename it with something more logical, like **b-blue**. The "Based On" window should show that its parent is **b**, and any revisions you make to **b** will be reflected in **b-blue**—except the overrides you made, in this example the character color.

Create a completely new character style

- With the Text tool, **T**, select the words that you want to add a character style to. Look to the Character Styles panel to see that "[None]" is highlighted.
- Using the same example, creating blue boldface text, open the Color window, either from the dock at right, or from the Window menu and choose "Color." If you also want the words or characters to be heavier, choose "Basic Character Formats" on the left and change the "Font Style" to a heavier weight.
- Once you've made these formatting changes, you won't see any difference in the Character Styles panel, with "[None]" still highlighted.
- At the bottom of the Character Styles panel, click on the Create New Style button, ⊞. This will add to the list a new style, named **Character Style 1**, that contains the formatting you just added, in this example the character color and font weight.

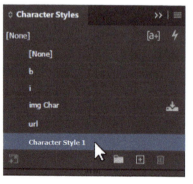

- Right-click on this new style to bring up the Character Style Options window, where you can rename it with something more logical, like **blue** or **bold-blue**. The

"Based On" window logically says "[None]"—you created this character style from applying formatting directly, not based on anything else.

Based-on styles

Basing a text style on another style is a powerful tool for adjusting text in your layout. In the ScML system, for example, most of the basic paragraph styles, like **paft**, **pcon**, **pf**, and **psec**, are based on the more fundamental **p** text style. If you adjust the point size or the font of the basic paragraph style **p**, all the related styles—like the first paragraph in a chapter (**pf**) or the first paragraph after a subheading (**paft**)—will update with the same formatting.

To see whether a text style is based on another style:

- Open the Styles panel and right-click on the text style name.
- From the menu, select "Edit." The Paragraph Style Options window appears, shown below.

The style name appears at the top, and below that "Based On." The "Style Settings" window shows what elements are different from the style it's based on.

In this example, we're looking at the Paragraph Style Options for **pcon**. This text style is used for the continuation of a paragraph after an interrupting element like a block quote.

The Style Settings box shows that two formatting settings make it different from the basic **p** text style: "+ first indent: 0 pt" means the first line of the **pcon** paragraph is not indented, and "space before: 16 pt" means the line space above a **pcon** paragraph is set to 16 points. If you adjust the indent or line space above for **p**, it won't carry over to **pcon**. But adjusting any other formatting element for **p**—font, point size, leading—will change the formatting for **pcon** too.

Adding a based-on style

If you have a text style that isn't connected to a more fundamental style, you can impose one in this Paragraph Style Options window.

- In the Based On box, select an existing text style. The Style Settings box will then populate with all the differences between the based-on style and the style you're editing.
- If you want to clean the slate, click "Reset to Base."
  This style will now have the same formatting as the based-on style. You can make the adjustments you need to differentiate this style from the based-on style. These will appear in the Style Settings box, and the formatting that's not listed will still be tied to the based-on style.

Disconnecting a based-on style

Sometimes a useful imported text style will be based on a not-so-useful style that you want to get rid of. Depending on the text style collection you are using, Microsoft Word's generic **Normal**, for example, might get imported as a parent text style. It's possible to disconnect a text style from the style it's based on.

- In the Styles panel, right-click on the name of the style you want to keep.
- Choose "Edit" to open the Paragraph Style Options window.
- In the Based On box, select "[No Paragraph Style]." All the formatting details of this style will now appear in the Style Settings box.

- If no other styles are based on **Normal**, you can delete it from the list in the Styles panel by selecting it and then clicking on the trash can at lower left, 🗑.

If the based-on style, in this example **Normal**, is disconnected from all the other text styles, it will just disappear. If any text style in the list is still based on **Normal**, or if **Normal** has been applied to any part of the manuscript, a dialog box will appear when you try to delete it, asking "Replace with" which text style? If you don't have the patience to figure out what it's connected to, it's easiest to just ignore it.

To verify that a formerly based-on style is no longer connected to other styles, you can use "Clean up unused styles" (page 70), explained below.

If you want to check whether the text style has been applied somewhere in the manuscript, use the text style search tool, described below in "Search for each instance of a text style" (page 70).

Useful text style tools

InDesign has a couple of other useful tools for working with text styles.

Load Text Styles

You can copy text styles from any other InDesign document. This can be useful if you've started a completely new document but want parts of it to look like one you worked on previously.

- In the Paragraph Styles panel, click on the top-right menu button, ▤.
- Select "Load All Text Styles."

Once you choose the InDesign document that contains the styles you want, a list of them appears. You can choose to import all of them, or only some of them. The formatting of the text styles you choose will overwrite any existing styles that have the same names.

Search for each instance of a text style

In a lengthy layout it can be useful to examine each instance of a text style to make sure it looks the way you want it to. InDesign's Find/Change function lets you jump through a layout to individual styles.

- In the Edit menu, select "Find/Change," or type CTRL-F or ⌘-F.
- In the Find/Change box, leave the "Find What" field blank. Below is the option to Find Format.
- At the right, click on the search button, 🔍.

The box that comes up lets you search for any text attribute, listed on the left side. If you wanted to find everything set in a specific typeface, for example, or a specific point size, you can use the options at left. On the right are the text styles—a pull-down menu of all the document's character styles, and a menu for all the paragraph styles. Selecting a text style and using "Find Next" will jump through the document, highlighting each instance of that text style.

Clean up unused styles

It's easy to find all the text styles that are not currently in use. This might be useful, for example, if you've disconnected a style from the style it was based on. You can find them all in one step:

- In the Paragraph Styles panel or the Character Styles panel, click on the top-right menu button, ☰.
- Click on "Select All Unused." The unused styles will be highlighted in the list.
- You can delete these unused styles all at one by clicking on the trash can at lower left, 🗑.

Sort the Styles panel list

In the Styles panel, you can get organized to find things more quickly by sorting the list of styles:

- In the Paragraph Styles panel or the Character Styles panel, click on the top-right menu button, ☰.

- Click on "Sort by Name." The list will reorder alphabetically.

Story Editor

Summon the Story Editor by first positioning the cursor in the text with the text tool 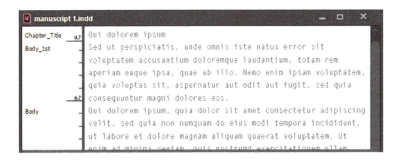, then selecting the Edit menu, and "Edit in Story Editor." The Story Editor window shows you all the text content in the layout, even if it's overflowing from a text frame and not visible, or hidden under an image, or set to be invisible.

The left side of the Story Editor window shows each paragraph's text style, and the text itself is on the right. The Story Editor will also point out errors like overset text, meaning when the text is overflowing and too long to fit in its text frame.

CSS for ebooks, websites, and digital content

Ebooks and websites use a version of text styles called cascading style sheets (CSS). CSS appears as a separate file in an ebook or on a website, and it sets out all the formatting—in addition to the way the text is formatted, it specifies visual styles, page layout and spacing, colors and background images. When you export a document from InDesign into the EPUB format, the most widely used for ebooks, the paragraph styles become styles in the CSS.

If you have an understanding of CSS and HTML, you can adjust how the document's text styles are exported to CSS and HTML format. In the Paragraph Styles panel, right-click on the name of a text style. From the menu that comes up, select "Edit." The Paragraph Style Options window appears. On the left side of this box, a list of all the formatting categories appears, including "Export Tagging" at the bottom. Here you can adjust how the text style is converted to HTML, and you can see the details of what the CSS for this style will look like.

About Henrietta Flores

Henrietta has worked in a variety of roles in journalism and publishing, through the industries' tribulations and contractions. Henrietta lives in California with a spoiled dog and a serious Scrabble addiction.

Index

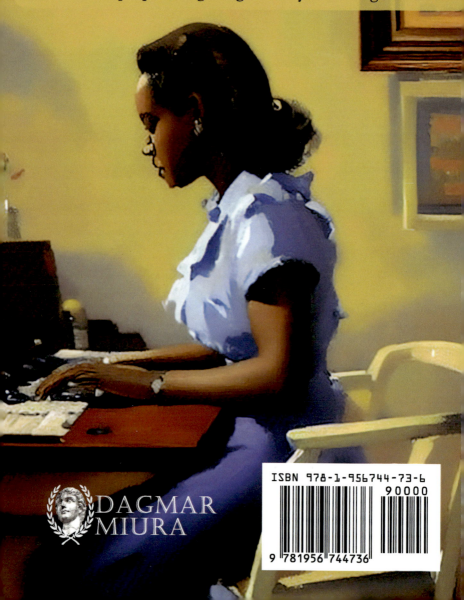

Working with the Text Styles that are built into the software we already use, we can simplify and speed up the process of turning a manuscript into a completed book or document. This guide is aimed at writers, editors, and designers who work freelance or in small organizations that don't have the resources to acquire beginning-to-end publishing systems. Using text styles removes the ambiguity of the intentions of writers and content creators, and saves the people doing design and layout from guesswork.

DAGMAR
MIURA

ISBN 978-1-956744-73-6

90000

9 781956 744736